A CONVERSATION WITH

SHAKESPEARE

READER'S THEATRE

 **DIANE BILYEU**

for
Theatre Productions USA

For school, church or home

A CONVERSATION WITH SHAKESPEARE

Published By:

DB Publishing
11076 N.Philbin Rd
Pocatello, ID 83201
1.208.241.8725

Produced by:

Book design, layout,
digital art, illustrations & cover: Ryan Roghaar

ISBN-13: 978-0-9800587-1-0
ISBN-10: 0-9800587-1-6

ABOUT THE AUTHOR

Diane Bilyeu has a degree in theatre and public speaking from Idaho State University. As an accomplished actress and professional dancer, Diane played many leading roles including Nellie Forbush in "South Pacific," Carrie Pipperidge in "Carousel," and Abigail in "The Crucible." She was also the leading lady in "Love Letters," "Plaza Suite," and "A Roomful of Roses" at Summer Stock in Sun Valley, Idaho.

Her love for the theatre and for children led the Bilyeus to buy a huge circus tent from Omar the Tent Maker in Los Angeles and produce plays in Bilyeu's Tent Theatre. All of these productions were musicals produced "in the round" and included at least three young children as performers. They had full houses every night of the week except when they were "dark" on Sunday and Monday.

Diane's husband "Chick," was a professor of theatre at Idaho State University. He was a graduate from the College of Theatre at the world famous Pasadena Playhouse in Pasadena, California. Chick went on to act professionally in several series and movies. In 2005, the Bilyeu's were honored for their work in education and theatre when the Proscenium Theatre at Idaho State University was named the "Diane and Chick Bilyeu Theatre." Diane still performs whenever possible.

Diane was also a professional dancer and traveled the entire United States for over a year. She returned home and taught dance to young children for many years. Diane's interest in children's education led her to becoming politically active and subsequently elected as State Senator. She was an active member of the Education Committee. This led to her appointment to the "Idaho State Board of Education" where she served for 10 years, several as president. Idaho State University, her alma mater, honored her with an honorary doctorate degree for her dedication to education.

Her love and strong belief in the importance of theatre for children has led Diane to create these plays. She believes self confidence, self-esteem, and reading fluency are natural outcomes when children perform in front of their families or peers. She has watched her own grandchildren develop as a direct result of performing in Reader's Theatre. She is also the author of Reader's Theater USA, a compilation of five original plays and a DVD.

The last time Diane's family gathered for Thanksgining they performed "A Conversation with Shakespeare." Her entire family participated aged eight to eighty. Twelve year olds took the parts of Romeo and Juliet. Eight, nine, and twelve year olds played servants and witches. Fifteen and seventeen year olds played interviewer, narrator, and Shakespeare. Fifty year old family members played Tybalt and Benvolio.

It was the best Thanksgiving ever. and her family looks forward to doing it again next year!

P.S. Diane just completed eight years as Idaho State Senator.

This book is dedicated to my late husband Chick, our three children Brigette, Clark, Valencia and nine grandchildren Aleksei, Taylor, Sterling, Lanni, Jackson, Winston, Halle, Cody and Aubri.

FORWARD

This play is written as an introductory celebration of one of the most fascinating figures of our past. It is intended to instill curiosity in students of all ages about the world's most celebrated playwright, William Shakespeare.

The script can be used at home, in church, or in the classroom. It is written for students with good reading skills. Children aged eight and up (including adults) can take part in the play. It will work best with around ten actors. Some actors will need to double up on parts, but that is part of the fun.

To make the experience a very special event, I suggest having an Elizabethan dinner prior to the play. This would include the entire audience or family. If presented for a larger group, it could be used as a fund raiser.

If you choose to have an Elizabethan dinner, keep the menu simple. First of all, no plates or utensils. You will need cups for the beverages. Let everyone eat with their fingers and pass the food down the table. I suggest chicken legs (KFC), vegetables (whole carrots, celery), fruit (grapes, oranges, apples), and whole loaves of French bread so that pieces can be torn off. For drinks I suggest ale, cider, lemonade, or just plain water. "Wenches" could walk around with baskets of fruit or bread. They could also help serve drinks. Damp wash cloths work great for napkins. Some festive music is also a nice touch. Just use your imagination and have fun!

At the end of the meal, have all participants assist in cleaning up the tables before starting the play. You may want to rearrange your tables to make room for the production.

CAST OF CHARACTERS

- Narrator

- Television Interviewer

- William Shakespeare

- Prince Escalus

- Romeo (Montague) (pronounced Mo´nt-a-gew)

- Juliet (Capulet)

- Tybalt (Capulet) (pronounced Tib'ult), Juliet's cousin

- Benvolio (Montague), Romeo's cousin and friend

- Servants, four

- Witches, three or four (I used the same actors for servants)

- Two audience prompters to lead cheering and change signs (could be done by Narrator)

A Conversation with Shakespeare © 2013 DB Publishing

PROPS AND COSTUMES

- COPIES OF SHAKESPEARE'S INSULTS FOR EACH AUDIENCE MEMBER!

- Two horns for opening of play

- Four music stands to hold scripts and signs

- Twelve marked scripts and light weight 3-ring black binders for each actor

- Regular street clothes for actors (other minimum costumes and props can be added as desired)

- Crown and robe (Prince Escalus)

- Berets, (optional for interviewer, Romeo, Tybalt, Benvolio)

- Seven belts (cording) to hold swords (Romeo, Tybalt, Benvolio, and four servants)

- Large cauldron (witches)

- Fake snake, toad, worm, entrails and stick to stir cauldron (witches)

- Three or four witches hats

- Seven plastic swords (Romeo, Tybalt, Benvolio, and four servants)

- One short dagger, one vial for poison, one small mask (Romeo)

- Two signs: "C" (for Capulets) and "M" (for Montagues), I put "CHEER" and "BOO" on back of signs.

OPTIONAL:

- Wig for Romeo, dark hair, no longer than shoulder length

- Wig for Juliet, any color, long, partly swept up on sides

STAGE LAYOUT

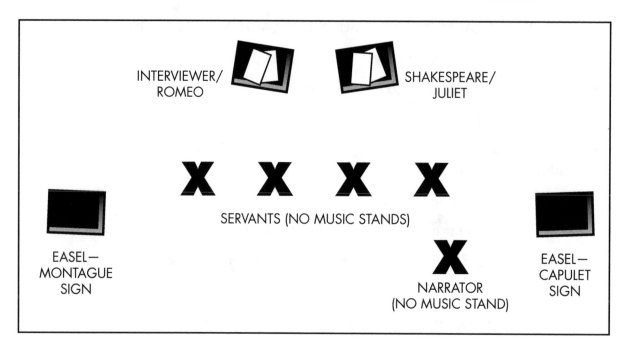

INTERVIEWER/
ROMEO

SHAKESPEARE/
JULIET

X X X X

SERVANTS (NO MUSIC STANDS)

X

NARRATOR
(NO MUSIC STAND)

EASEL—
MONTAGUE
SIGN

EASEL—
CAPULET
SIGN

POINTERS FOR THE DIRECTOR

1. Provide a copy of "Shakespearean Insults" (included at end of script) for each participant, both audience and actors.

2. Each actor playing a part should have his or her own script that is 3-hole punched and placed in a light-weight binder.

3. Have the auditioning actors read the play aloud. Then with their help, cast the play.

4. Give each cast member a script and help them underline or highlight their lines. If the director wants to save time, the highlighting or underlining could be done prior to distributing the scripts. Be sure stage directions are not highlighted; we don't want the actors to read directions aloud.
    The technique of highlighting or underlining helps actors locate their lines while reading from the printed page. Also circling the character's name in red is an easy way to locate their place in the script. You may also circle any instructions.

5. Read through and mark the script. Have the actors sit in a circle holding their scripts for the first read-through. This is the time to start marking the script, so provide highlighters and pencils. If an actor wants to emphasize a word, underline it. If they want to remember a pause, draw slash marks (/////) or an exclamation mark. These are great interpretive reminders and will be very helpful at performance time.

A Conversation with Shakespeare © 2013 DB Publishing

POINTERS FOR ACTORS

1. Describe your character. Ask questions such as: what kind of background did the character have? Was the character happy, rich, devious, dishonest? This kind of analysis will help in your character development. Remember, you are playing someone else, not yourself.

2. Always stay in character. Be sure your body movement is in character, too.

3. "Pick up" your cues – there should be no time lag between lines. In fact, sometimes, if the action is fast, you may want to talk over the end of another actor's lines. Your director can help you with this timing.

4. Never make eye contact with an audience member. This breaks the magic of your part and therefore affects the play. When looking towards the audience, look over their heads.

5. Speak your lines loudly and clearly, pushing air from your chest, not from the back of your throat. Project or direct your voice to the back of the room. This is one of the most important points for actors: Projection, projection!

6. Take your time and speak clearly. Do not rush your speeches. Remember, this is the first time your audience has heard the story. Give them the chance to understand what you are saying.

7. When the audience laughs at your lines, be sure you "hold," or wait for a few seconds, until the laughter starts to die out, then continue your dialogue. Whatever you do—don't laugh with the audience!

8. Whenever you can, look at the actor who is speaking, unless of course your part calls for you to look the other way.

9. In Reader's Theatre, try to keep your finger on your place in the script. That way, if you have time to look at the other actor who is reading a part, you can find your place again immediately.

10. The key to oral reading is enthusiasm and volume! Your eyes, voice and body should sparkle each time you read – animation, animation! Even though you have read the same part many times as you rehearsed, remember that this is the first time for your audience and they deserve your very best performance. They should believe that you are the character, not just acting. Put yourself completely into the part you are reading.

11. Curtain call, where the audience "thanks you" with their applause, is a special time. Even though you probably will not have an actual curtain, you will still want to do a curtain call. Actors may take their bows alone, as couples or as an entire cast together. It's up to you and your cast. Be as creative as possible.

When it's the entire cast, I like them to line up across the front of the stage, hold hands, raise them up in the air and bring them down to at least the knees as they bow. What fun the curtain call and the applause is for both actors and audience! It is the actors' reward for having done a good job.

As they say in the theatre world: "Break a leg!" (Actors consider it bad luck to say "good luck" to one another before a show). HAVE FUN!

And now: "ON WITH THE PLAY!"

A Conversation with Shakespeare © 2013 DB Publishing

A CONVERSATION WITH SHAKESPEARE

ACT 1

(The stage should already be set with four music stands. The two used for signs should already have the signs stacked on them and items (props) , should be close by, perhaps on a chair at side of staging area).

TRUMPETERS: *(Enter playing horns and then loudly say)* Hear ye!! Hear ye!!, the play is about to begin! Shakespeare is coming! Shakespeare is coming! Come and listen to "A Conversation with Shakespeare"! *(trumpeters leave staging area playing horns)*

NARRATOR: *(Enters with a flourish saying)* Good day *(good morrow, good afternoon)*, ladies and gentlemen, and welcome.

Today we are presenting for you a readers theatre style two-act play called *(pause)* "A Conversation with Shakespeare."

Our cast is made up of all of you, because this day you will become part of our play! So let's begin. As the Bard would say, "the play's the thing!"

(Narrator leaves stage. ACT I opens as television interviewer enters and places script on music stand. Invterviewer speaking In a loud and overbearing way)

INTERVIEWER: Good evening ladies and gentlemen, and welcome to KQBS-TV right here in Hollywood, California. You might ask yourself, "What does KQBS stand for? Well, it stands for the King's and Queen's Broadcasting Station, not the King's and Queen's Baloney Station, as some of you might think.

INTERVIEWER: Today we have as our invited guest none other than England's most famous bard, story teller, poet and playwright, Mr. William Shakespeare. Not only did he write at least 36 plays which included comedies, tragedies, and histories, but he also introduced some of the best phrases, new words and insults that I have ever heard.

Ladies, gentlemen and groundlings, while we are waiting for the "Bard," Mr. Shakespeare, to arrive, I want to get you in the mood for a little Elizabethan fun.

Oh, by the way, let me explain what groundlings are. They were the audience members who stood on the ground in front of the stage. Actually, it's the best place to see the play, but they had to stand there - no seats for the groundlings!

Now we are going to try a little experiment with those of you in the audience. I am going to divide you into two groups. This side of the audience will be called the Capulets (place "C" sign on designated side of room on music stand), and this side the Montagues (place "M" sign on other side of room on other music stand).

We will be discussing and doing a few scenes from "Romeo and Juliet" today and that is why I am naming you the Capulets and Montagues. You also will be taking part in our short version of that play. These signs will help you remember who you will be cheering for.

The Capulets are Juliet's family. The easiest way for me to remember that Juliet is a Capulet is to visualize her with a cap on her head—got it? Cap on head, Capulet, Juliet. Let's hear it for the Capulets! Come on Capulets, a little louder!

A Conversation with Shakespeare © 2013 DB Publishing

(interviewer points to Capulet side and leads applause for the Capulet side)

INTERVIEWER: Then we have the Montagues who are Romeo's family. Remembering Romeo's friends will be easy if you just remember their names all end with an "o." Like Benvolio or Romeo. It helps because there are a lot of people in Shakespeare's plays. Now let's hear it for the Montagues! Come on Montagues a little enthusiasm!

(interviewer points to Montague side and leads cheering for the Montagues)

Now, remember I mentioned the great insults that Shakespeare wrote? Well, each of you will be given papers listing Shakespearean insults. Take a quick look at them and when I say "GO," I want the Capulets to go to the Montagues and start shouting insults at them from those lists.

At the same time, the Montagues are to shout insults back at the Capulets using your Shakespearean insult sheets. This is what I call The Battle of the Insults!! Could I have some of the wenches or other assistants hand the insults to our guests?

(Interviewer, assisted by "wenches" and others, hands each audience member the Shakespearean insults. To save time for larger groups, they could also be placed ahead of time face down at each place setting and INTERVIEWER could call audience attention to the sheets)

So, ladies and gentlemen, Using the Bards own words, I beseech you all to begin insulting each other! GO!

(AUDIENCE as Montagues and Capulets, interact with insults. After about three minutes, Interviewer begins in a loud voice)

INTERVIEWER: Ladies and gentlemen thank you, you have insulted each other with great fervor and passion – well done! But, I have just been told that the Bard, William Shakespeare, is about to enter the studio.

Capulets and Montagues, please hand in your insult papers and return to your seats, or if you are groundlings, to the ground. Thank you, thank you!

(AUDIENCE returns papers and take seats or sits on the ground.)

And now, ladies and gentlemen, please rise and help me welcome, direct from London, England, the most famous playwright in the world, the greatest storyteller that ever lived, the one and only - Mr. William Shakespeare!

(Enters with a flourish, takes off his hat as he bows)

SHAKESPEARE: Good morrow, kind gentlefolk, and thank you for your most gracious welcome to the United States of America! Even though I am British, I'm quite glad you won your independence from England. We were being very unfair to you, wanting you to pay all those taxes from afar. Of course, if you were still British and had paid those taxes, I would now be considered your playwright, too.

INTERVIEWER: Well, we welcome you, Mr. Shakespeare, and even though we are Americans and not British, we think of you as a citizen of the world. Your plays are performed all over the world and in many languages; and so, we think of you as America's playwright, too!

SHAKESPEARE: Thank you very much. I did not realize it at the time, but yes, my plays have lasted a long time, haven't they? I did write some pretty good plays and poetry, wouldn't you agree?

INTERVIEWER: Yes you did, and they have inspired not only the stage, but movies, music, art and literature.

SHAKESPEARE: Well, I am very proud of what I wrote over 400 years ago. Quite frankly, I'm amazed they have retained their popularity.

INTERVIEWER: Your plays are timeless and translated all over the world. I think your friend Ben Johnson said it best about you. He said, and I quote, "He was not of an age, but for all time."

SHAKESPEARE: He said that? Well, that was very kind of him. I wasn't sure he cared for me or for my writing.

INTERVIEWER: Do you mind sir, if I ask you a few personal questions about both your life and your writings?

SHAKESPEARE: I don't mind at all. Go ahead, please. I will try to answer your questions.

INTERVIEWER: First of all, would you tell us about your family life?

SHAKESPEARE: Certainly, I was born in Stratford-Upon-Avon in England in 1564. I married my sweet Anne Hathaway in 1582. I was 18 years old and she was 26, eight years older than I.

INTERVIEWER: Wow, that was quite an age difference. What did people say?

SHAKESPEARE: Not much really. She was quite lovely and a very good wife. I traveled a lot you know, being in the theatre, and it was hard to get back home to Stratford from London. Anne was very patient with all my travels.

INTERVIEWER: Did you have children?

SHAKESPEARE: Oh yes, we had three children. Susanna was our first and then we had twins, Hamnet, not Hamlet, and Judith.

INTERVIEWER: I like those names.

SHAKESPEARE: But my dear son Hamnet died when he was only 11 years old. He was the apple of my eye. The boy was humorous, full of love and a wonderful student.

INTERVIEWER: I'm very sorry sir. That must have been devastating. He sounds like he was a wonderful son.

SHAKESPEARE: He was, and I am sure Hamnet would have been a fine actor and playwright had he lived. Or, he might have been a glove-maker like my father, John. It absolutely broke my heart when Hamnet died. Maybe that's one of the reasons I was able to write so many tragedies. His death was a tragedy for me.

INTERVIEWER: I'm sure it was. Didn't you write most of your tragedies after your son's death?

SHAKESPEARE: You are a very observant Shakespearean scholar. You know a lot about my feelings, my life and my writings. Yes, I wrote "Hamlet," "Othello," "King Lear" and "Antony and Cleopatra," all after his death.

INTERVIEWER: I have been doing a lot of research about you, sir.

SHAKESPEARE: Well, don't believe everything you read or hear!

INTERVIEWER: Don't worry, I won't. But tell us about your education in Stratford. Were you a good student? Did you like school? What was it like?

A Conversation with Shakespeare © 2013 DB Publishing

SHAKESPEARE: We went to school very long hours, from eight in the morning until six at night. We had very few holidays. It was very rigorous. We studied Latin, Greek, French, and Italian; we translated and read aloud. I'm proud to say I was quite proficient in Latin.

INTERVIEWER: That is very interesting, thank you for sharing some of your personal life with us. However, if I might change the subject, I would like to ask you a few questions about your writing.

SHAKESPEARE: Go ahead, please.

INTERVIEWER: First of all, why did you never include women as actors?

SHAKESPEARE: Good question. Of course, in those days women were not allowed to take part on the stage. They were permitted to attend plays, but not to be actors.

INTERVIEWER: That seems so unfair!

SHAKESPEARE: I didn't think anything about it at the time. But now that you mention it, it was quite foolish. Of course it gave me great difficulty in writing and directing my plays. I did write some pretty good female parts, but had to find young boys before their voices changed, to play the female roles.

INTERVIEWER: That brings another question to my mind, sir.

SHAKESPEARE: You are welcome to just call me Will.

INTERVIEWER: Oh, I honor you way too much to just call you by your first name, sir. So, I will just continue to call you Mr. Shakespeare. Tell me, why did you have so many witches and ghosts in your plays?

SHAKESPEARE: Oh my, how the audiences loved my witches, spirits, ghosts, dreams, and bad omens. If a scene was getting a little bogged down, I'd just put in a few witches or let one of the characters have a bad dream telling of something horrible that might happen in the future.

INTERVIEWER: You did write some great witch scenes. I love the witches in Macbeth!

SHAKESPEARE: I thought of it as "tricks of the trade." My audiences loved them and would often cheer or boo for the witches. However, people were very superstitious in those days. Many of them actually believed in witches, bad omens and spells that might be cast.

INTERVIEWER: Wow, that is so interesting! I thought it might be something like that. In fact, I have a few actors who would like to show you their interpretation of your witches from "Macbeth." Would you be so kind as to watch them?

SHAKESPEARE: I would be delighted! Of course, "Macbeth" is my shortest and most gruesome tragedy. It is a wonderful story of a noble war hero who turns into a murderer. The witches are getting ready for Macbeth's visit. He is coming to ask them what the future holds. Go ahead, please.

(Three witches enter cackling, bent over, and looking fertively around. They are carrying a cauldron and stick, snake, toad, worm, and entrails. As each item is dropped into the cauldron, hold it high so the audience can see what it is.)

(Witch 1 putting cauldron down and starting to stir)

WITCH 1: Round about the cauldron go.
In the poison entrails throw. *(Hold up/drop into cauldron)*
Toad, that under cold stone *(Hold up/ drop into cauldron)*
Days and nights has thirty-one.

Sweltered venom sleeping got
Boil thou first in the charmed pot.
(Cackling and stirring)

ALL WITCHES: Double, double, toil and trouble;
Fire burn, and cauldron bubble.
Cool it with a baboon's blood
Then the charm is firm and good

WITCH 2: Fillet of fenny snake, *(Hold up and drop in snake)*
In the cauldron boil and bake;
Eye of newt and toe of frog, *(Hold up and drop in frog)*

WITCH 2: Wool of bat and tongue of dog,
Adder's fork and blind worm's sting, *(Hold up and drop worm)*
For a charm of powerful trouble,
Like a hell-broth boil and bubble. *(Still stirring and cackling)*

ALL WITCHES: Double, double, toil and trouble;
Fire burn, and cauldron bubble.
By the pricking of my thumbs, *(Feels thumbs)*
Something wicked this way comes. *(Shout)*

IT'S MACBETH! *(All witches leave cackling, take cauldron)*

SHAKESPEARE: (Applauds) Very well done! The witches are wonderful
and evil creatures.

I loved writing for the witches and the audiences went
crazy for them. Sometimes one of the groundlings would
even jump on stage and try to stir the cauldron!

INTERVIEWER: Thank you witches. Just a few more questions.
Mr. Shakespeare. Have you seen the Globe Theatre in
London?

SHAKESPEARE: Which one are you speaking of? I was part owner of the first Globe. It was glorious! It had a thatched roof made of straw; thatching was very popular in those days.

INTERVIEWER: Thatched roofs are beautiful.

SHAKESPEARE: Yes, they are. Unfortunately, during a performance of "Henry VIII," a spark from the stage cannon accidentally caught the roof on fire. In just one hour, the glorious Globe burned to the ground.

INTERVIEWER: How awful. Was anyone injured?

SHAKESPEARE: Luckily no. One man's trousers caught on fire, but a friend poured his bottle of ale over him and put it out.

INTERVIEWER: Sounds like a good use for some of that ale!

SHAKESPEARE: We were able to rebuild the Globe in about a year; but this time, we used tile for the roof instead of straw thatching. The new Globe was just as successful as the old one. We could, and did, play to at least 2,000 people at a time.

INTERVIEWER: Wow, that's a lot of people! Another question I'm curious about, how much money did playgoers pay to see a play in those days?

SHAKESPEARE: The "groundlings," those who stood around the stage, paid only one pence; the richest people sat in the Lord's room and paid six pence and then there were those who paid three pence for benches. I made very good money as an actor, part-owner and playwright.

INTERVIEWER: The Globe must have been fascinating.

A Conversation with Shakespeare © 2013 DB Publishing

SHAKESPEARE: It was. The plays were done in the daytime you know. We had no electricity for lights like you have now. Audiences stood in line with food and drink to see our plays. Sometimes they would even boo or throw food at the actors, if they disliked a performance. Water was unsafe to drink so many became a bit tipsy after drinking their ale.

INTERVIEWER: How did you collect money for your plays?

SHAKESPEARE: We had "gatherers" standing at the doors with boxes to collect admission. They would gather money and put it in their boxes; that is why you now call your ticket office the "box office." Did you know that?

INTERVIEWER: No, that's a bit of trivia I missed in my Shakespeare reading. I'm glad we don't have "gatherers" with boxes gathering money outside the theatre now.

SHAKESPEARE: Of course, our second Globe with the tile roof was also destroyed. It was torn down in 1644 by the Puritans during England's Civil War. They thought theatre was evil. It was after my death, but it makes me sad to hear about it now.

INTERVIEWER: Did you know a third Globe has been built again, in London almost exactly where your Globe stood. It is glorious and was made possible because an American actor, Sam Wanamaker,was in London and saw only a plaque where your Globe had been. He spent the rest of his life committed to rebuilding your famous playhouse, and it is beautiful.

SHAKESPEARE: I'm happy that an American cared that much about the Globe and my plays. I would like to see it when I go back to London. I might even see one of my plays there.

INTERVIEWER: Tell us about your favorite plays.

SHAKESPEARE: "Macbeth" is one of my favorites. It is sooooo bloody and full of witches, ghosts, premonitions and murder! Definitely not one to see just before you go to bed. It was wonderful to write. I must tell you, I would sometimes sneak into the theatre and observe the audiences. I loved hearing them laugh, boo or cry.

INTERVIEWER: What are your other favorites.

SHAKESPEARE: Well, I love "Othello;" partly because of the interracial love complications and of course, Iago (Pronounced Ee-AH-go), the villain, is a wonderful role for an actor. One of my other favorites was my first real tragedy, "Romeo and Juliet."

Then there was "King Lear," and "Merry Wives of Windsor" with the well-loved character, John Falstaff. I delighted in some of the names I gave my characters, names like Puck and Bottom. Can you imagine naming one of your children "Bottom?" Those names still make me laugh!

INTERVIEWER: You did write some great plays! Mister Shakespeare, sir, some of our actors have a short scene from "Romeo and Juliet." They would like very much to show it to you. Do you have time?

SHAKESPEARE: Of course! I love that people are still acting and reading my plays.

INTERVIEWER: The actors are having a bit of fun with your play, so please don't be offended. I hope you are ready for some American hams.

A Conversation with Shakespeare © 2013 DB Publishing

SHAKESPEARE: I'm flattered. Let the American version of "Romeo and Juliet" begin.

INTERVIEWER: Sir, I beg your leave to join the cast of actors.

SHAKESPEARE: Please go right ahead. I may take one of the parts myself.

(Interviewer and Shakespeare take scripts and leave the staging area. They could take another part if needed.)

(Narrator enters and goes to music stand on either stage right or left, looks up at audience and with dramatic pause says.)

THE TRAGEDY OF "ROMEO AND JULIET"

(Short pause)

Two households, both alike in dignity,
In fair Verona, where we lay our scene,
From ancient grudge break to new mutiny,
Where civil blood makes civil hands unclean.

From forth the fatal loins of these two foes
A pair of star-cross'd lovers take their life;
Whose misadventured piteous overthrows
Do with their death bury their parents strife.

The fearful passage of their death-mark'd love,
And the continuance of their parents' rage,

(Narrator leaves and puts up signs that say "cheer or boo")

(2 Capulet servants enter and go to front of stage)

CAPULET SERVANT 1: (in loud whisper to SERVANT 2) Draw thy tool; here comes two of the house of Montagues.

(Both servants take out swords and motion for Capulet audience to cheer)

CAPULET SERVANT 2: My naked weapon is out. (Speaks to SERVANT 1) Quarrel; I will back thee.

CAPULET SERVANT 1: How? Turn thy back and run?

CAPULET SERVANT 2: I will frown as I pass by and let them take it as they list.

CAPULET SERVANT 1: Nay, as they dare, I will bite my thumb at them; which is a disgrace to them, if they bear it. (Bites thumb)

(2 Montague servants enter)

MONTAGUE SERVANT 1: Do you bite your thumb at us, sir?

CAPULET SERVANT 1: I do bite my thumb, sir. (bites thumb again)

MONTAGUE SERVANT 2: Do you bite your thumb at us, sir?

CAPULET SERVANT 1: (Aside to CAPULET SERVANT 2) Is the law of our side, if I say ay?

CAPULET SERVANT 2: No!

CAPULET SERVANT 1: No, sir, I do not bite my thumb at you sir; but I bite my thumb, sir. (Bite thumb again)

CAPULET SERVANT 2: Do you quarrel, sir?

MONTAGUE SERVANT 1: Quarrel, sir! No, sir.

CAPULET SERVANT 1: But if you do, sir, I am for you: I serve as good a man as you.

MONTAGUE SERVANT 2: No better.

CAPULET SERVANT 1: Well, sir.

A Conversation with Shakespeare © 2013 DB Publishing

CAPULET SERVANT 2: (Aside to CAPULET SERVANT 1) Say 'better,' here comes one of my master's kinsmen.

CAPULET SERVANT 1: Yes, better, sir.

MONTAGUE SERVANT 1: You lie!

CAPULET SERVANT 1: Draw, if you be men. Remember thy swashing blow.

(All four servants put down scripts and fight with swords. Servants interact and encourage audience to cheer or boo)

(Benvolio enters with sword drawn, beating down the servants weapons)

BENVOLIO: Part, fools! Put up your swords; you know not what you do.

(Servants continue fighting, enter Tybalt, sword drawn)

TYBALT: What, art thou drawn among these heartless hinds? Turn thee, Benvolio, look upon thy death.

BENVOLIO: I do but keep the peace, put up thy sword or manage it to part these men with me.

TYBALT: What, drawn and talk of peace! I hate the word, as I hate hell, all Montagues and thee. Have at thee, coward!!

(TYBALT and BENVOLIO drop scripts and fight. SERVANTS continue fighting and AUDIENCE cheers or boos! Enter Prince Escalus)

PRINCE ESCALUS: Rebellious subjects, enemies of peace, profaners of this neighbor-stained steel, will they not hear? What, ho! You men, you beasts. On pain of torture from those bloody hands, throw your mistemper'd weapons to the ground, and hear the sentence of your moved prince.

(All weapons are thrown to ground and servants step to side so prince is in middle of staging area)

Three civil brawls, bred of an airy word by thee, Capulet and Montague, have thrice disturb'd the quiet of our streets. If ever you disturb our streets again, your lives shall pay the forfeit of the peace. For this time, all the rest depart away; you, Capulet, *(To Tybalt)* shall go along with me; and, Montague *(To Benvolio)*, come you this afternoon, to know our fathers pleasure in this case. Once more, on pain of death, all men depart!

(Tybalt, Benvolio, Prince ESCALUS exit)

(FOUR SERVANTS pick up scripts, move front of stage and break into rap song)

MONTAGUE SERVANTS:

Yeah, yeah, yeah, yeah!
We don't need a prince to tell us what to do!
Cuz nuthin's better than a Montague!

CAPULET SERVANTS:

Now, now, now, now!
You just don't get it, and I'm surprised
We're the Capulets and we despise!
So, show us what you got! Show us what you got!

MONTAGUE SERVANTS:

Yeah, yeah, yeah, yeah!
Hold on a minute you capulets!
Put your thumbs away, and let's forget!
Tell us what you want, tell us what you want!

CAPULET SERVANTS:

Now, now, now, now
We can't explain it, we're wastin' our time
Wastin' our time, wastin' our time!

(Montague and Capulet servants together)

Yeah, yeah, yeah, yeah!
There's nothin' better than a family feud
Nothin' better than a family feud!
Say it again boys, say it again!
There's nothin' better than a family feud!
YEAH!! (hands point out to audience)

(All servants take scripts and swords and leave. Narrator enters and goes to front of stage either right or left. Center stage is left for Romeo and Juliet.)

NARRATOR:

And so it was decreed by the prince himself, that anyone in Verona who continued age-old feuding between the Capulets and Montagues would be banished, or their lives would be forfeited.

At the end of Act 1, Romeo and his friends decide to attend a costume party at the Capulets. It is a masked ball and they don carnival clothes and masks to crash the party.

(ROMEO and JULIET enter and go to music stands where Shakespeare and Interviewer stood. ROMEO sees JULIET and falls madly in love with her and she with him)

ROMEO:

What lady's that, which doth enrich the hand of yonder knight? O, she doth teach the torches to burn bright! For I ne'er saw true beauty till this night. (Romeo removes mask)

NARRATOR: After Romeo talks directly to Juliet, she is smitten with him. They exchange loving and witty words until she is called away. Juliet then learns his name and says:

JULIET: My only love sprung from my only hate! Too early seen unknown, and known too late!

NARRATOR: Later that evening, Romeo, unable to stay away from Juliet, climbs over the Capulets' orchard wall. He overhears her speaking.

JULIET: O Romeo, Romeo! Wherefore art thou Romeo? Deny thy father and refuse thy name. Or, if you wilt not, be but sworn my love, and I'll no longer be a Capulet... What's in a name? That which we call a rose by any other word would smell as sweet...

NARRATOR: Romeo lets Juliet know he is there and the lovers talk until dawn.

JULIET: Romeo?

ROMEO: My dear?

JULIET: At what o'clock tomorrow shall I send to thee?

ROMEO: At the hour of nine.

JULIET: I will not fail: 'tis twenty years till then. I have forgot why I did call thee back.

ROMEO: Let me stand here till thou remember it.

JULIET: I shall forget, to have thee still stand there, remembering how I love thy company.

A Conversation with Shakespeare © 2013 DB Publishing

ROMEO: And I'll stay, to have thee still forget, forgetting any other home but this.

JULIET: 'Tis almost morning; I would have thee gone. Yet no farther than a wanton's bird, who lets it hop a little from her hand.

ROMEO: I would I were thy bird.

JULIET: Sweet, so would I; yet I should kill thee with much cherishing. Good night, good night! Parting is such sweet sorrow, that I shall say good night till it be morrow.

(ROMEO and JULIET both leave the stage parting reluctantly)

NARRATOR: The lovers part reluctantly and Juliet has agreed to meet Romeo the next day and be secretly married. Friar Lawrence agrees to marry them and hopes that with this marriage the long standing quarrel between the Capulets and the Montagues will end.

           After the marriage, Juliet hurries home and waits for Romeo to meet her once more in the orchard. About noon, Benvolio comes across Tybalt and a group of Capulets; a quarrel begins.

(Benvolio and Tybalt enter and begin pantomime)

(Tybalt argues with BENVOLIO [pantomime a lot of pushing, hand gestures etc.] until Romeo enters and tries to stop the fight)

TYBALT :   Romeo, thou art a villain!

NARRATOR: Benvolio and Tybalt draw their swords and begin to fight. Romeo is trying to avoid any quarrel and tries to reason with them both, but his efforts only hinder Benvolio who receives a fatal wound.

(BENVOLIO falls to the ground and dies dramatically)

NARRATOR: Romeo now avenges his friend's death and begins a sword fight with Tybalt. (Narrator pauses while fight occurs and until Tybalt starts to fall to ground) Romeo kills Tybalt!

(Tybalt falls to the ground and also dies dramatically) (Romeo very upset, leaves stage area)

NARRATOR: (After Romeo leaves staging area) Romeo is now banished from Verona. The Capulets, in the mean time, not knowing that Juliet is married to Romeo, are still insisting that she marry Count Paris, the man they have selected for her.

Juliet consults Friar Lawrence and they hatch a plan for her to take a powerful drug that will make her appear to be dead. (Juliet enters and lies down on back on floor as if she is in a tomb) She will then be taken to the family tomb because everyone will think she is dead, but of course she is just in a deep sleep. The Friar tells her of his plan for Romeo to arrive as Juliet awakens and he can then take her to Mantua to live happily ever after. Unfortunately, Romeo never gets the message; and upon hearing of Juliet's death, buys a dram of poison and hurries back to Verona. The timing is not good; and when Romeo arrives at the tomb, he finds Juliet appearing to be dead.

(Narrator pauses while Romeo sees Juliet and goes to her)

Romeo then kisses Juliet, drinks the poison, and falls by her side. Juliet awakens and sees the body of Romeo. Wanting nothing more from life, Juliet takes Romeo's dagger, stabs herself and falls mortally wounded by his side. (Narrator pauses until Prince Escalus arrives and then says.) Prince Escalus is first upon the tragic scene and calls for the Capulets and Montagues.

A Conversation with Shakespeare © 2013 DB Publishing

PRINCE ESCALUS: (Standing in middle of dead bodies) Capulet!
Montague! See, what a scourge is laid upon your hate,
that heaven finds means to kill your joys with love! And
I, for winking at your discords too, have lost a brace of
kinsmen; all are punish'd.

NARRATOR: Then the Capulets and the Montagues reconcile at last.
So deadly had been their rage and enmity in the past,
nothing but the death of their beloved children could
remove this bitter hatred and jealousy.

PRINCE ESCALUS: A glooming peace this morning with it brings;
(Pauses and raises hand) The sun for sorrow will not show
his head:

Go hence, to have more talk of these sad things;
Some shall be pardon'd and some punished.
For never was a story of more woe

Than this of Juliet and her Romeo.

(All actors and narrator quietly leave stage. Shakespeare
and Interviewer go back to original places.)

SHAKESPEARE: That was excellent. I am so glad that my words have
lasted for so many years; and I loved, what did you call it,
the rap song!

NARRATOR: Yes, Mr. Shakespeare, rap is a new rage in America.

SHAKESPEARE: Thank you, thank you so much, but it is time for me to
leave you now. I have another interview in New York
City and then I am off to Paris and then to Tokyo. "All
the world's a stage" you know, and they do love me in
other parts of the world. But none of them will be as heart-
warming and make me feel as welcome as you have here.

SHAKESPEARE: (To AUDIENCE) Please ladies and gentlemen, be kind to each other and always remember my words, "to thine own self be true." ADIEU! ADIEU! FAREWELL!!

(SHAKESPEARE leaves with a flourish)

INTERVIEWER: Adieu to you also, Mr. Shakespeare, and thank you. (Turns to AUDIENCE) And of course a very special thank you to our actors, and to you our studio audience. ADIEU, ladies and gentlemen, and please remember, in the words of William Shakespeare, "All the world's a stage, and the men and women merely players. They have their exits and their entrances, and one man in his time plays many parts."

And now, from KQBS in Hollywood, California, GOODNIGHT!!

(Entire cast enters, holds hands and takes a big curtain call to wild applause from audience.)

A Conversation with Shakespeare © 2013 DB Publishing

NOTES

NOTES

SHAKESPEAREAN INSULTS

Choose one phrase from the list below and fill in the blank with your choice of words from the adjacent page.

The tartness of your face sours ripe grapes, thou _____

Out, you green-sickness carrion! Thou art _____

Detested parasites, thou art _____

There is not ugly a fiend of hell as thou art, you _____

Your breath first kindled the dead coals of wars, _____

Thou speak'st false, thou art _____

Upon the next tree shalt thou hang alive, thou art _____

Thou smell of mountain goat. Thou art _____

Out of my sight! Thou art _____

Thou dost infect my eyes! Thou art _____

Hide not thy poison with such sugar'd words. Thou _____

My tongue will tell the anger of my heart! Thou _____

Out, you baggage! You tallow face! Thou art _____

I was searching for a fool when I found you! Thou _____

A Conversation with Shakespeare © 2013 DB Publishing

Clay-brained	Red-tailed bumble bee
Flap-ear'd	Mad-headed ape
Puking	Jolt head
Fat-kidneyed	Vagabond
Hook-nosed	Villain
Bag-seed	Ingrate
Gluttonous	Nut-hook
Quarrelsome	Cretinous puff bag
Ill-favoured	Peasant
Logger-headed	Strumpet
Deformed	Toad
Flap-dragon	Scullion
Lily-liver'd	Mad-cap
Conceited	Weasel
Puppy-headed	Ninny

SERVANTS RAP SONG

(MONTAGUE SERVANTS)

YEAH, YEAH, YEAH, YEAH!

WE DON'T NEED A PRINCE TO TELL US WHAT TO DO!

CUZ NUTHIN'S BETTER THAN A MONTAGUE!

(CAPULET SERVANTS)

NOW, NOW, NOW, NOW!

YOU JUST DON'T GET IT, AND I'M SURPRISED

WE'RE THE CAPULETS AND WE DESPISE!

SO, SHOW US WHAT YOU GOT! SHOW US WHAT YOU GOT!

(MONTAGUE SERVANTS)

YEAH, YEAH, YEAH, YEAH!

HOLD ON A MINUTE YOU CAPULETS!

PUT YOUR THUMBS AWAY, AND LET'S FORGET!

TELL US WHAT YOU WANT, TELL US WHAT YOU WANT!

A Conversation with Shakespeare © 2013 DB Publishing

(CAPULET SERVANTS)

NOW, NOW, NOW, NOW

WE CAN'T EXPLAIN IT, WE'RE WASTIN' OUR TIME

WASTIN' OUR TIME, WASTIN' OUR TIME!

(Montague and Capulet SERVANTS together)

YEAH, YEAH, YEAH, YEAH!

THERE'S NOTHIN' BETTER THAN A FAMILY FEUD

NOTHIN' BETTER THAN A FAMILY FEUD!

SAY IT AGAIN BOYS, SAY IT AGAIN!

THERE'S NOTHIN' BETTER THAN A FAMILY FEUD!

YEAH!!

(Hands point out to audience)

RAP
SONG

A Conversation with Shakespeare © 2013 DB Publishing

Printed in the USA
CPSIA information can be obtained
at www.ICGtesting.com
LVHW070007210224
772409LV00011B/531